FAVOURITE
TROUT
AND
SALMON
RECIPES

compiled by
Margaret Ashby

Illustrated with
fly-fishing scenes by
Briggs RI

LMON

Index

Front cover picture: "Trout Fishing in Galloway"
Back cover picture: "Loch Lundy and Ben Tee"
Title page: "The Gentle Art"

Printed and Published by J. Salmon Ltd., Sevenoaks, England © Copyright

Notes on Cooking Game Fish

Preferably eat freshly caught fish as soon as possible, but, if they are to be frozen, clean and freeze without delay. All the best fishing hotels provide freezing facilities, as do some large reservoirs.

There is no substitute for butter in the cooking of game fish, and even in these cholesterol conscious days, it is still the only thing to use. Nothing else is quite right in either flavour or texture.

If cooking with wine, a good dry wine is definitely the best, usually the one chosen to drink with the meal.

Herbs are very important in fish cookery and here again, ones collected

The Headwaters of the Dochart

fresh from the garden, just as they are needed, have no substitute. They are so easy to grow, even in a small courtyard. When serving cold smoked salmon or trout at a party, serve from a bed of freshly picked herbs. Fennel or dill are good as they will keep the bread moist and add a decorative touch. Don't forget to garnish with parsley, which is a 'must' for any fish dish, the crisper and greener the better.

For fish stock, freshly made is best, using bones, heads and tails but fish stock cubes, readily available, are an excellent substitute.

Trout caught in waters that have a muddy taste can be improved by soaking in salt water with a good dash of wine vinegar. Leave for 2-3 hours and then dry and treat as normal trout. It is perhaps a good idea to be a little more generous, however, with the lemon juice or wine when cooking such fish. These fish do need to be scaled, as the scales can hold the muddy flavour.

Never spoil game fish cookery with malt vinegar. Wine vinegar is better. Dry cider can be quite a good alternative.

Sea salt is better than cooking salt.

Fresh ground pepper is a 'must'. Nutmeg and mace are the best spices.

As for frozen game fish, it is better to defrost in the refrigerator, leaving the fish wrapped in its packing. A rough guide is 18 hours for a fish weighing up to 4 lbs, and 24 to 36 hours for a medium-sized whole fish. If you are pushed for time leave the fish at room temperature allowing 4 hours per pound. Steaks and cutlets can be cooked from frozen, but allow a longer cooking time.

A final word about presentation of cooked fish to the table. Some cooks have recommended that the skin should be removed. Do leave the skin on. It helps to keep the flesh moist, and connoisseurs usually think it a necessary part of the dish.

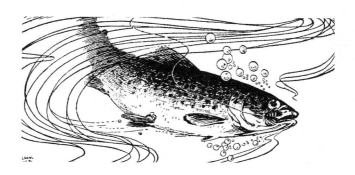

Baked Stuffed Salmon (or Sea Trout)

The joy of being married to an angler is seeing the beautiful fish caught (and dispatched immediately), and presenting it whole to family and friends. It should look just as elegant cooked as it did alive.

4-5 lb. sea trout, salmon or trout
¼ lb. fine breadcrumbs, soaked in milk   2 anchovy fillets pounded, or essence
4 oz. sautéd pink mushrooms   Fresh herbs of your choice, finely chopped
Salt and pepper to taste
(Prawns can be substituted for anchovy fillets and sliced green olives are an interesting option)

Clean and dry the fish, wipe the cavity with lemon juice or tarragon vinegar. Squeeze excess milk out of the soaked breadcrumbs and add the finely chopped herbs, sautéd mushrooms and the butter they were cooked in. Traditionally anchovies are added next, but especially for sea trout with their delicate flavour, prawns may be used as an alternative, depending upon taste. Season to taste, mix well and stuff the cavity with the mixture. If on the dry side add another knob of butter. Secure with cocktail sticks. Wrap in oiled foil and place on baking tray or dish. Cook in a preheated oven 375°F or Mark 5 for 45 minutes. Test with a fork to ensure it is cooked as ovens vary so much. May be served with a lemon sauce.

Baked Salmon with Oyster Stuffing

*Salmon are just beautiful to eat and look at, but the combination
of oysters with salmon is to die for.*

Tail end of fish weighing 2-3 lbs. and filleted
Fresh Oysters or a tin if fresh ones are not available
1 heaped tablespoon finely chopped parsley
4 oz. fine breadcrumbs   4 oz. butter   1 egg yolk beaten
2 glasses dry white wine   ¼ pint double cream
Good pinch nutmeg   Ground mace (a good pinch)
Seasoning to taste

Put the oysters in a bowl complete with the liquid. Add the parsley, bread-crumbs, seasoning and spices. Beat into this mix 3 oz. of the butter and the egg yolk. Prepare the fillets and lay flat. Spread the mixture over one half. Do not go too near the edge. Place second fillet on top, and secure with kitchen string, to keep the filling in place. Put the fillets in a baking dish, dot the remaining butter and seasoning on top. Cover with foil. Bake in a hot oven at 400°F or Mark 6 for about 45 minutes. When cooked place on a warm serving dish. Add the cream to the liquor and stir in. Pour this over the fillets. Serve at once, removing the string first. Small new potatoes and possibly barely cooked sliced green beans, go well with this lovely dish.

Celebration Salmon, Sea Trout or Trout

This dish is just what it's name says it is – in our house we have a celebration at the drop of a hat – just catching a good fish for instance.

**1 salmon, sea trout, or trout, about 3 lb. is ideal   ½ pint of double cream
2 glasses dry champagne or a dry sparkling wine   Seasoned flour
1 cucumber cut into neat cubes   Butter for cooking**

Clean and gut the fish and wipe dry. Butter well an ovenproof dish, lay the prepared fish in and spoon or brush the thick cream over fish. Sprinkle the seasoned flour over cream. Place in a preheated oven at 375°F or Mark 5 and cook for 5 minutes. Take out of oven and baste well. Give another 5 minutes, baste again and then add wine (champagne really is worthwhile) any remaining cream and cook for a further 30/40 minutes according to size. Baste at intervals. Taste for seasoning at this point, adjust if necessary, and stir sauce if necessary. Meanwhile poach the cucumber cubes in salted water for 5 minutes. Do not let them lose their colour. Drain and keep hot. Cucumber cubes sauted in butter is an alternative. If serving from an oven dish, you can add the cucumber to the cream sauce. If not, decorate the serving dish with cucumber, lift fish out very carefully and spoon sauce over fish and vegetable. As fish come in all shapes and sizes, cooking times are very difficult to give. The times given are guidelines only. Champagne is the drink for this fish, and if it really is the fish of a life-time, then it must be worth it.

The Tay below Stobhall

Salmon en Croûte

This recipe is ideal if you need some extra padding for good appetites.

Sea trout or grilse (ideally 3 lbs. in weight)
1½ lb. puff pastry (ready made or frozen can be used)
2 oz. butter   2 oz. breadcrumbs, soaked in milk   1 lemon   Seasoning
1 teaspoon of ground mace   4-6 oz. prawns or shrimps, sautéd
Sprigs of as many fresh herbs as possible including tarragon

Clean and gut the fish, and skin. Put on one side and make the pastry (if frozen or ready made pastry not used). Roll out as thinly as possible, slightly longer than the fish and about three times as wide. Leave to rest while making stuffing. Squeeze breadcrumbs to get rid of surplus milk. Add finely chopped herbs reserving 4 sprigs of the tarragon whole. Work in butter and put in salt, pepper and mace. Beat well. Stuff cavity of the fish with this mixture. Place fish in the middle of the puff pastry and brush flesh with double cream. Put sprigs of herbs on the cream. Sprinkle fish with salt and pepper. Carefully fold pastry round the fish. Either decorate with pastry fish shapes or make the join as decorative as possible. Press the pastry as tightly as can be round the fish. Place on baking tray and bake in a hot oven at 400°F or Mark 6 for first 20 minutes. Reduce heat to 350°F or Mark 4 and cook for a further 25-30 minutes. If getting too brown cover with foil. To serve, place on flat dish and decorate with the prawns, lightly sautéd and lemon cut in slices.

Baked Sea Trout

Sea trout, if anything, is superior to salmon, but has become very scarce. Loch Maree in the Highlands was the magical place to catch them but sadly this is no longer the case.

1 sea trout 3-4 lbs. in weight
Fresh herbs, fennel, thyme, tarragon, chives, etc.
Seasoned flour
Butter

Butter a cooking dish and lay some of the herbs on the base. Clean the fish and pat dry, rub the seasoned flour all over the outside, season the inside and pop some more fresh herbs and a knob of butter in cavity. Lay in the dish over the herbs, cover with buttered foil, and cook in a preheated oven at 350°F or Mark 4 for 30 minutes. Remove foil and cook for a further 10 minutes to crisp the flavoured skin. This is ideal hot or cold, but if serving hot, pour juices over, and remove the herbs before serving. Excellent with browned almonds. If served cold, lemon mayonnaise and fresh cucumber complement the flavour of the fish.

Trout in Herb Cream

*Cream and herbs go with just about everything – especially fish,
and game fish even more so – enjoy!*

1 small trout per person   ¼ pint milk   ¼ pint cream
2 oz. white breadcrumbs   3 oz. butter
Sprigs of tarragon or fennel per fish
1 tablespoon of finely chopped mixed herbs (tarragon, chives, thyme, parsley, etc)
Seasoned flour

Clean the trout, and rub over with the seasoned flour. Place in a buttered dish, placing a sprig of fresh herb inside each fish with a little knob of butter, from the given amount. Pour the milk into the dish, and cook in preheated oven, covering with foil or lid. Bake at 400°F or Mark 6 for 20-30 minutes depending on size of fish. Take out of the oven, add the chopped herbs to the cream, and stir into the cooking liquid. Sprinkle the breadcrumbs evenly over each fish and dot with the remaining butter. Place under a hot grill for long enough to brown the crumbs, and the cream to bubble. Serve from the cooking dish.

Stuffed Trout Cooked in Vine Leaves

*Stuffing fish ensures that the extra flavours in the stuffing
get through to the delicate taste of the trout.*

**4 trout (1 lb. or less)   ½ lb. butter
½ pint shrimps (cut in half)   Salt and pepper to taste   Pinch of mace
4 sprigs of either fresh tarragon or lemon thyme
Vine leaves for wrapping, well buttered and wiped over with lemon juice or wine vinegar**

Clean the trout well and gut. If you are expert at emptying the gut through the gills, this leaves a nice pocket for the stuffing to stay intact. Place a sprig of herb in each fish. Mix the butter, mace and shrimps together, season with the salt and pepper and divide into 4 portions. Place a portion in each fish. Squeeze any lemon juice over on the fish. Wrap each trout in vine leaves, covering completely. Secure with kitchen string. Place in an oven dish, buttered lightly. Cook in hot oven at 375°F or Mark 5 for ¾ hour, with either a foil covering, or lid. Serve with crisp parsley, lemon slices and (ideally) really small new potatoes, well minted. Our local delicatessen sells Greek vine leaves in brine. They are bigger than English ones, but slightly tougher and they do need to be washed to get excess salt out. If using fresh leaves, blanch in boiling water for 1-2 minutes.

Savoury Baked Trout

*Trout is a very versatile fish, and the delicate flavour is just perfect
for whatever is added to it, as here with this savoury dish.*

Fillets of trout up to 3 lbs.   1 onion, chopped finely
½ green pepper, sliced   1 clove garlic, crushed
½ lb. chopped tomatoes   2 bay leaves, crumbled
4 rashers of bacon   Dash of Worcester sauce, to taste
Butter for frying

Fry the chopped onion in the butter. When just transparent throw in the
pepper, and garlic. When these have turned colour slightly, add the chopped
tomatoes, and bay leaves. Cook for 5 minutes over heat. Add Worcester sauce.
Line a shallow dish with the bacon rashers. Put the fish fillets on top of these
neatly, then cover with the hot vegetables. Bake in hot oven 375°F or Mark 5
for 45 minutes.

Trout Rosé

This recipe is as good to look at as it is to eat, just try it.

Trout   Bottle of dry Rosé Anjou or a light dry red
3 shallots, finely chopped   Bay leaves   Sea Salt   Black pepper
Butter for cooking and for sauce   2 or 3 cloves, optional   1 oz. flour

Defrost the trout if using frozen, and 3-4 hours before cooking, butter an earthenware or glass cooking dish. Lay the trout in it. If one trout only, pop 2 bay leaves in the cavity and season, or 1 bay leaf per small fish. Chop the shallots very finely and sprinkle over and around the trout. Cover with the Rosé or light red wine, season, and put in a cool place, turning fish over every hour. Set oven to 350°F or Mark 4 well before needed. Cover the dish carefully with a tight-fitting lid or foil, and put in preheated oven. Timing will depend on size of fish. If small one of say ¾ lb give 25 to 30 minutes. A larger fish up to 1½ lbs will need 40 to 45 minutes. When cooked, lift out carefully onto serving dish and keep hot. For sauce, melt 1 oz of butter in pan, and stir in 1 oz of flour. When blended, pour in the wine the fish was cooked in, stirring all the time. Cook gently for 3 minutes, and if too thick add wine until right consistency, heated right through. The sauce should have a faint blush. Pour the sauce over fish. Serve with creamed potatoes. As it is an autumn or even winter dish, try some tinned artichoke hearts, slightly sautéd in a little butter.

Whisky Trout

Fish and whisky seem made to go together and with good reason.
The water that started the whisky off is probably the same water the trout came from.

4 trout (small ones preferably)   ¼ lb. butter
Crushed clove garlic   Salt and pepper to taste
Chopped green onions, 1 per fish   Chopped parsley (I use a lot)
1 tablespoonful grapeseed oil
1 large measure of whisky

Butter an oven dish evenly, and put aside. Mix the oil, salt, pepper, and crushed garlic and brush this over the trout, both sides. Put into the oven dish, and sprinkle with parsley and chopped onions. Dot with remaining butter. Pour the whisky evenly over the fish. Cook in preheated oven 375°F or Mark 5 for 30 minutes, basting at least twice during cooking time. To make sure the fish is cooked, test with a fork. This can also be done in a frying pan. Serve with lemon slices.

Trout Kedgeree

Kedgeree takes us back to India, where perhaps the fish were not quite as fresh as we are used to, so curry and spices made it palatable. Those days are passed, but this still makes an excellent dish.

1½ lb. trout poached in salt water	**3 hard boiled eggs**
2 cups of cooked long grain rice	**Butter for cooking**
2 large onions, sliced	**Seasoning**

Poach the trout. When trout is cool enough to handle, skin and remove the bones and flake the flesh. Put on one side. Butter an ovenproof dish 12" x 8" x 2", and put a layer of sliced onion on the bottom. Cover this with a layer of the cooked rice, sprinkle half the trout on this, covered by the finely chopped egg white, put flakes of butter on top of this and season with freshly ground pepper and salt. Repeat layers, ending with the hard boiled yolks grated as the final layer. Season again and dot with butter. Cover with grease proof paper, to ensure the rice does not harden. Cook in preheated oven at 350°F or Mark 4 for 30 minutes to cook onion and heat everything thoroughly. Serve at once from dish. Chopped parsley is the only garnish needed as the layers make it a very attractive dish to serve.

Foil-baked Fish
(Especially Sea Trout and Grilse)

Cooking fish in foil ensure all the delicate flavours and juices are preserved.

1 sea trout or other weighing approx. 3 lbs.-5 lbs.
Squeeze of lemon   Seasoning
1 oz butter   Oil for foil

Clean and gut the fish, remove all blood from cavity, and brush inside with lemon juice. Flake the butter and spread evenly inside and season. Use a large piece of foil (oiled) and place fish in the centre. Make a secure parcel by wrapping the fish and twisting the ends of the foil. Although you don't want it to leak, it is better to have a loose parcel. Place on baking tray and cook in preheated oven at 375°F or Mark 5 for 40-50 minutes, or longer according to its size. Remove from the oven and allow 15-20 minutes for fish to rest. Open parcel carefully, and place fish on serving dish, when cool enough to handle. If it is to be garnished, remove uppermost skin while still warm.

Trout in Orange Sauce

Trout and salmon can be adapted to go with most things so try this orange sauce recipe. It makes a change from the more usual lemon.

2 trout under 1 lb., or 1 large trout 1½ lb.   2 oz. butter
Sage, chives, and lemon thyme, or herbs of own choice
Seasoned flour   Rind of 2 large oranges and 5 ozs. of juice
Breadcrumbs (about 2 ozs.)   Butter for cooking

Clean and gut the trout carefully, and wipe dry. Put the butter and breadcrumbs into a bowl and wipe oranges carefully, taking care not to release the zest. Then finely grate as much of the peel into the bowl as possible. Season the mix and add the very finely chopped herbs or dried herbs. Beat all together. Spread this mixture evenly into the cavity of the fish (if too dry, add a little fresh orange juice, enough to make a smooth, not liquid, paste). Cut oranges in half and extract every bit of juice. Put the fish into a well buttered dish, dredge lightly with seasoned flour, and pour orange juice over. Dot fish with flakes of butter. Put into preheated oven at 350°F or Mark 4 for 20 to 35 minutes according to size. Cover with a lid of foil, but baste at least 3 times during cooking. The butter, flour and orange juice make a lovely sauce. Leave uncovered for the last 10 minutes. If the oranges did not have enough juice, add some unsweetened orange from a carton to make up to the required amount. Serve with creamy potatoes and very fresh watercress.

Poached Salmon (or Trout)

We had a very ancient fish kettle for poaching our fish,
I think it came from my mother-in-law, but it is not essential.

1 salmon cleaned and gutted, any size as long as it fits into kettle
Bouquet garni   White wine (dry) bottle   Celery stalk, chopped
2/3 carrots, chopped   1 onion, sliced   3 bay leaves
Blade of mace   Few peppercorns, lightly crushed   Salt to taste

Put the fish into the kettle. Pour the bottle of wine over first, then top up with cold water, to ensure the fish is covered with liquid. Throw in the chopped vegetables and spices. Bring the contents to the boil and then simmer for three minutes. Remove from the heat at once and allow to cool naturally. Lift the fish out carefully when cold, remove skin leaving head and tail intact. Garnish as required.

If the fish is to be eaten hot, for the initial cooking a 6-7 lb. fish will need to simmer for about 20 minutes, then be removed immediately from the liquid and served. But as fish come in all sizes it is a problem to know exactly how long to cook them for. The fork test is probably the best way of telling when they are done. If you are lucky enough to have landed something akin to the Loch Ness Monster the only way to do it justice is to leave the tail end for poaching, and use the rest for cutting into steaks or stuffing. Experiment with as many recipes as possible.

Breakfast Salmon

Trout and salmon are so versatile they can be eaten for any meal;
breakfast just as easily as lunch or supper.

Salmon steaks with skin on   **Oatmeal**
Beaten egg   **Butter for frying**
No seasoning traditionally

Wipe the steaks and dip in the beaten egg. Have the oatmeal on a plate. Dip the egged steaks into the meal making sure the egged sides are well covered. Heat the butter in the pan. When bubbling (but not brown) put steaks into pan and cook for 10 to 12 minutes according to thickness. Turn once. Traditionally these were not to be seasoned or have any fancy sauce with them. However,· as with grilled salmon steaks, you may prefer a squeeze of lemon, but I am not sure that does anything for the oatmeal. Small trout from the stream can be cooked in a similar way, and larger trout can be filleted and also cooked in the same way; and a very good meal it is too.

Trout with Almonds

Almonds with trout is a classic recipe, they complement each other so well.

4 trout (small ones are quite good for this recipe)
4 oz. butter   4 oz. almonds, flaked
Seasoned flour   Lemon juice

Wash and clean the trout and pat dry. Rub all over with the flour until coated. Heat the butter in a pan until it is bubbling and fry the trout 4-5 minutes on each side. When ready, put on a dish to keep hot. Add more butter to the pan if necessary and fry the almonds until golden brown, no more. Cover the fish evenly with the almonds and keep warm. Add the juice of a large lemon to the butter which the fish and almonds were cooked in and just bring to the boil. Pour over the fish at once. Serve on a dish garnished with fresh parsley. The nice thing about fried trout is that the skin is so delicious and it is a pleasure to eat it when crispy and golden.

Trout in Oatmeal

Living in Scotland, fish, whisky and oatmeal (porridge with whisky and cream is superb)
just go together. This is my favourite breakfast when on holiday in Scotland.
My husband catches and cooks the fish.

2 small trout per person coarse oatmeal
Butter for frying   Salt and pepper
Diced bacon, 1 rasher per brace of fish (optional)

Clean the trout, slit open and remove the backbone. Season the oatmeal with salt and pepper, then coat the fish, covering all over with the meal. If bacon is to be used, fry diced bacon until slightly crisp. Remove from the pan and keep warm. Heat the butter in the pan, mixing in with the bacon fat. When bubbling but not brown, put in the trout. Cook on both sides until golden brown. Serve with parsley and diced bacon, or lemon wedges if the bacon is not required.

Smoked Salmon Tarts

These little tasty tarts are so useful, for parties, picnics, starters or lunch.

24 baked pastry cases	**Juice of a lemon**
8 oz. smoked salmon pieces	**lemon slices**
4 oz. butter	**Pinch of cayenne**
2 tablespoons best mayonnaise	**Seasoning**
2 tablespoons sour cream	**Parsley sprigs**

Blend the salmon and butter together, then beat in lightly the sour cream, mayonnaise and lastly the lemon juice. Taste before adding salt and use freshly ground pepper. Fill each case with mixture. Cut lemon slices and place on each tart before serving. Sprinkle very lightly with a pinch of cayenne over the tarts – just a whisper. Add a sprig of parsley on each tart.

Smoked Salmon Quiche

When I had a large family I would make what my mother always referred to as savoury flans. It is always worth making two, one for the freezer.

1 cooked pastry case
¼ lb. scraps of smoked fish (the more the better, obviously)
½ pint cream   3 egg yolks   Salt and pepper to taste   Mace, powdered
Anchovy essence (if smoked fish very sparse)   Cayenne pepper, few grains
Fresh parsley, finely chopped (or tarragon)
Any cold fish (trout or salmon best) if available for extra filling

Cut the smoked fish into even-sized pieces (thumb-nail size). Beat the egg yolks and add to the cream. Season to taste with salt, pepper and mace. Add the anchovy essence if being used. Mix in the herbs and the smoked fish and any cooked fish. Pour into the pastry case, making sure the fish is evenly distributed. Bake in a moderately hot oven at 350°F or Mark 4 for about 45 minutes or until cooked. Sprinkle with cayenne. Alternatively, you can use small pastry cases. Cooking time for these tartlets is 30 minutes at the same temperature as above. Small new potatoes, well buttered, sprinkled with either chopped parsley or scissored chives are ideal to serve with the quiche. A very simple side salad with a good crisp lettuce like Webbs or Iceberg, is really all that is needed, unless you have some tender asparagus which is even better.

Smoked Trout or Salmon Flan

What I cooked depended on what my husband had caught, but trout are obviously easier to come by and we did have a mini smoker.

Rich shortcrust pastry	**1 egg, beaten**
8 oz. smoked trout/salmon	**Seasoning**
4 oz. pink mushrooms	**Pinch of mace**
¼ pint cream	**Butter for frying**

Roll out the pastry thinly and line a shallow flan case, but reserve enough for a lid. Slice the mushrooms thinly and fry lightly in the butter. Flake the fish into small pieces and beat into the egg. Add the cream, the mushrooms and the butter they were cooked in, the seasoning and mace. Mix well. It should not be too runny. Put into the pastry case and cover with a lid. Bake at 375°F or Mark 5 for 35-40 minutes. Garnish with lemon slices and fresh parsley.

Smoked Trout Mousse

We always found children, as well as adults, like this.
It is easy to eat – no bones, and delicious.

4 smoked trout fillets, boned and skinned
½ pint soured cream
1 tablespoon of hot horseradish sauce

1 sachet gelatine
Juice of 2 lemons
Freshly ground black pepper

Flake the trout flesh and mix with the sour cream. Dissolve the gelatine in the lemon juice, and stand the cup in a bowl of boiling water to melt. When liquid, add to fish mixture, beat well, with the horseradish and black pepper to taste. If bulk is needed, the well beaten white of an egg will certainly increase the volume without losing any flavour. Pour into a suitable mould. Chill in the fridge, or alternatively this will freeze well. To serve, turn out of mould, dipping into hot water if necessary. Garnish with watercress or cucumber, and serve with brown hot toast. As smoked trout is salty anyway, don't add salt unless tasted beforehand, and found wanting. A variation this recipe stands up to very well is to substitute cottage cheese for the soured cream.

Smoked Trout Paté

*Patés are so easy, I think you can make it almost while the toast is doing,
unless you make the toast in front of an open fire; it tastes better!!*

1 large smoked trout (2 fillets)   **1 crisp apple (we use Granny Smiths)**
¼ lb. butter   **Juice from 2 lemons**
¼ pint soured cream   **Freshly ground black pepper**

Skin and bone the fish if necessary and flake with a fork. Soften the butter for
easy mixing. Grate the apple and cover with the lemon juice, to keep its colour.
If a blender is to be used, put all the ingredients in and blend until smooth. I
beat until well mixed but not too smooth. Serve with a simple crisp salad and
brown bread and butter. Add more lemon if required, although the lemon in
the pate should be sufficient. Watercress (if fresh) would be as good as a salad
and does add visual appeal.

Salmon (or Trout) Vol-au-Vents

*I like to have these for family times such as Christmas and Easter. I have quite
a large family so a batch of these handed round, whilst keeping an eye on the main meal,
are very handy and go down well with a glass of wine.*

**1 lb. puff pastry (frozen will do if you are busy) or ready prepared vol-au-vent cases if liked
½ lb. cooked and neatly flaked trout or salmon   ¼ pint double cream
½ pint very thick béchamel sauce, with grated nutmeg   ¼ lb. pink mushrooms
1 glass of dry sherry or white wine   24 prawns, cooked   Fresh parsley sprigs for garnish
Butter for cooking mushrooms   Salt and pepper
Bake pastry cases and allow to cool.
(Quantities given are enough for 24 cases).**

Melt the butter in pan until bubbling. Add the neatly sliced mushrooms and
just lightly saute. Add the mushrooms and flaked fish into the still warm
béchamel sauce. Add the cream beaten with sherry (Manzanilla with its
slightly salty taste seems to go so well with fish). Season to taste. Fill the vol-
au-vents with this mixture. Do not be afraid to taste for seasoning, and adjust
for personal taste. Pop a shelled prawn on top of each filled vol-au-vent before
putting on a lid at an angle to show prawn beneath. Put into an already heated
oven 300°F or Mark 2 for 5 minutes. Decorate with a small parsley sprig on
each case.

Salmon in Red Wine

Red wine is not the usual choice for salmon, but it is interesting, try it.

6 salmon cutlets (or one per person)   **¼ pint fish stock (stock cube if necessary)**
6 evenly sized mushrooms (optional)   **¼ pint double cream**
½ pint red Burgundy   **Salt and pepper to taste**
Butter for cooking

Well butter a thick frying pan. Have cutlets of even size. Place in the pan, and cover with the Burgundy, and very gently poach until cooked, being very careful not to break them. Place on a warmed serving dish. Add the stock to the wine the fish was cooked in, and simmer until reduced to approximately ½ a pint. Pour the cream into this liquid and bring to the simmer. Don't let it boil. Season to taste, strain and pour over the cutlets. Top each one with lightly sautéd mushroom if using them. Serve with a nice green vegetable *al dente*, (sliced green beans or mange tout peas go well) and very creamy mashed potatoes, garnished with finely chopped parsley or chives.

Suffolk Trout

I grew up in an old Tudor farmhouse in Suffolk but my father was a Scot, so I have a foot in both camps. I knew several of the locals, and they cooked mackerel like this.

4 trout
2 oz. butter
4 bay leaves   Juice of a lemon   Seasoning

Clean and gut the trout and take the heads off. Pop a bay leaf inside each fish with a twist of pepper and salt. Melt the butter in a thick frying pan. Put the trout in when the butter is bubbling. Add the lemon juice over fish. Cover, turn heat down and cook slowly, turning once. Serve very hot with petit pois and either small potatoes or potato balls tossed in a little butter. Garnish with parsley.

Salmon and Asparagus Flan

Asparagus has such a short season, so we have to make the most of it – no better way than with salmon. Don't forget, the off-cuts of asparagus will be good with soup.

Good shortcrust pastry shell
½ lb. cooked salmon   2 eggs
½ lb. asparagus, cooked lightly, 3 minutes at most
½ pint single cream
Finely cut bulbs of spring onions
Pinch of mace   Seasoning

Make a good shortcrust pastry and bake blind in an 8 inch flan case. Beat the eggs and cream together. Bone and skin the salmon, flake, and add to the eggs and cream. Season and add mace. Keep four spears of the cooked asparagus and cut the rest into ½ inch pieces. Add these to the mixture with the finely chopped onion bulbs, and pour into the flan case, putting the whole spears decoratively on last. Bake in a hot oven at 375°F or Mark 5 for 35-40 minutes. Smoked salmon pieces can be used instead of fresh salmon and is equally good. Just freshly boiled potatoes, garnished with finely-snipped chives, is all you need to accompany this dish, but a crisp green salad is never amiss.

Trout or Salmon Soup

I make soup, any time, and with anything that's handy, but fish soups I love.

1 pint of fish stock or more if you have it (you can always freeze surplus soup)
Check for seasoning   1 stalk celery, chopped   1 leek, very finely sliced
¼ lb. small mushrooms, thinly sliced (pale ones)
¼ pint of shelled shrimps or halved prawns   5 oz. dry white wine or sherry   2 oz. butter
2 heaped tablespoons of flour   Cupful of leftover trout or salmon
Fresh parsley, thyme or tarragon   Seasoning to taste if necessary

If no fish stock available, very good fish stock cubes are available. Put the stock into saucepan. Melt butter in frying pan (don't let it colour, only bubble). Add the vegetables and cook for 3-4 minutes. Strain the vegetables, leaving as much of the butter in the frying pan as possible. Add the vegetables to the stock, bring to the boil and simmer for 10 minutes. Now add the fish and prawns or shrimps and bring back to the simmer. Stir the flour into the butter in the frying pan and mix well over low heat. When blended add the wine and stir carefully. Tip this very carefully into the soup and when blended perfectly simmer for no more than 4 minutes. Decorate with fresh herbs. Serve with croutons. I think it is preferable to have the pale mushrooms for eye appeal, the dark looking ones just don't seem to go with the delicate colour of the soup.

Spiced Trout

*Having a constant supply of trout, we did like to experiment,
and we liked it spiced. A very good starter.*

Cold cooked trout, preferably fillets
½ pint of wine vinegar
1 teaspoon of cloves
½ teaspoon of allspice
8 peppercorns
Sea salt to taste

Mix all the ingredients (except fish) in a saucepan and boil for 2 minutes. Leave to cool. Strain and pour over fish. Put in a cool place for at least 2 hours. Drain. Serve with a crisp salad.

Potted Trout

Potting food is the traditional way of preserving meat or fish before fridges were thought of, but it still works very well today.

½ lb. cold trout or salmon   ¼ lb. butter
Good pinch of salt, pepper and mace
Anchovy essence to taste (I use about a dessertspoon)

Flake the cooked fish, remove bone and skin. Either beat or put all ingredients into blender for 2-3 minutes (or until smooth). In cold weather just soften butter first for easy mixing. Put into attractive dish if serving straight away, or suitable container for freezing. Cover with melted butter. Chill or freeze. Cover with foil if freezing. Serve with brown bread, toast, or hot rolls.

Wiltshire Grayling

Grayling are hard to come by, but an angler lucky enough to catch one will never forget it, so cooking has to be worthy of this fish.

4 small grayling
3 oz. hazelnuts, chopped
Juice of I lemon
½ oz. of butter
Seasoned flour
Grapeseed oil for frying

Clean and gut the grayling. Remove the scales. Coat with the seasoned flour. Heat the oil in thick frying pan and when hot, cook grayling 4-5 minutes each side. Transfer to a warm serving dish and keep hot. Put the butter and lemon juice in the frying pan. When bubbling add the chopped nuts, turn them till brown. Don't let the butter burn. Pour over fish. Serve with creamy potatoes.

Grilled Fresh Salmon Steaks

We were given this simply delicious dish by a very sweet Scots woman.
Quick to prepare and with a good fish there is no need to tart it up.

Salmon steaks one inch thick
Salt and pepper to taste
Melted butter for brushing over the steaks
Serve with lemon and parsley butter

Heat the grill on high for 2-3 minutes before grilling salmon. Brush the cutlets with melted butter, season to taste. Always use freshly ground pepper. Cook the salmon under the hot grill for 3-4 minutes only each side, brushing the underneath side and seasoning before putting back under the grill. Can be eaten with just a squeeze of lemon, but it is worth preparing some parsley butter if it is for a dinner party.

Trout/Salmon Pancakes

We usually allow two thin pancakes per person and do not use sugar but only grated lemon rind.

Cold poached trout or salmon
¾ pint béchamel sauce with 2 tablespoons of tomato sauce
¼ pint of double cream   2 oz. butter
Grated Parmesan cheese (optional)   Salt and pepper to taste

Make pancakes in the normal way. Do make them thin, like crêpes. Keep them warm. Meanwhile heat butter in frying pan until bubbling, not brown. Turn the flaked trout in the pan until heated through. If you don't want to use the cheese you can at this point add a spoonful of herbs (tarragon, chives or parsley). Halve the béchamel sauce and put one half in the pan with the fish. Stir well, being careful not to break the fish up too much. Divide this mixture equally between the number of pancakes made. Put the pancakes on hot dish and keep hot while the covering sauce is made. Add the cream to the remaining béchamel sauce. Add the seasoning and tomato sauce and bring almost to the boil. Pour over the pancakes and serve immediately, unless using the parmesan cheese, in which case sprinkle cheese evenly over the pancakes and flash under a hot grill for just long enough for the cheese to colour slightly. Serve at once, garnished with finely chopped fresh parsley.

METRIC CONVERSIONS

The weights, measures and oven temperatures used in the preceding recipes can be easily converted to their metric equivalents. The conversions listed below are only approximate, having been rounded up or down as may be appropriate.

Weights

Avoirdupois	Metric
1 oz.	just under 30 grams
4 oz. (¼ lb.)	app. 115 grams
8 oz. (½ lb.)	app. 230 grams
1 lb.	454 grams

Liquid Measures

Imperial	Metric
1 tablespoon (liquid only)	20 millilitres
1 fl. oz.	app. 30 millilitres
1 gill (¼ pt.)	app. 145 millilitres
½ pt.	app. 285 millilitres
1 pt.	app. 570 millilitres
1 qt.	app. 1.140 litres

Oven Temperatures

	°Fahrenheit	Gas Mark	°Celsius
Slow	300	2	150
	325	3	170
Moderate	350	4	180
	375	5	190
	400	6	200
Hot	425	7	220
	450	8	230
	475	9	240

Flour as specified in these recipes refers to plain flour unless otherwise described.